The Waiting Room

A 31-day Daily Devotional for Single
Women Waiting for the
Right Husband

T.C. SPELLEN

The Waiting Room:
A 31-day Devotional for Single Women Waiting
for the Right Husband
Copyright 2012 T.C. Spellen
TCS Publishing
Brooklyn, NY
www.tcspellen.com

ISBN-13: 978-0615759746
ISBN-10: 0615759742

Cover Design by: Jose Castañeda

Proofreading by: Marleen Harris-Jasper,
Karen Powell and Karen Young

Manuscript Editing by: Joy Sillesen
www.indieauthorservices.com

Book design by: Maureen Cutajar
www.gopublished.com

Dedication

This is dedicated to all women who desire and simply deserve unconditional and authentic love.

ACKNOWLEDGEMENTS

I'd like to thank my heavenly Father – the giver of life and dreams – who planted *The Waiting Room* into my belly. I'd also like to thank the Golden Door Spa and Resort for providing the perfect environment to receive the idea and format of this book with clarity.

Thank you to my parents for always believing in me. A special thank you to my mother, Annette L. Spellen, my best friend, bodyguard and promoter. Thank you for loving and supporting me ALWAYS. You are AWESOME and I love you!

Thank you, Rev. Valerie E. Cousin, for leading, mentoring, and befriending me. It's because you selflessly invested time in me and other women that I'm familiar with spiritual disciplines and have made them a lifestyle. This book is the product of many hours of training under your tutelage and sisterhood, and I'm grateful.

Thank you to my accountability partner, Jazzmine Clarke-Glover, who took her assignment seriously.

To ALL of my sisters: thank you for your love, support, and patience. I've talked about writing a book for about twenty years, and all of you encouraged me to *walk in my dream*. Thank you for the confidence you had in me; it certainly exceeded the confidence I had in myself.

CONTENTS

INTRODUCTION

Welcome to the waiting room. This is a 31-day devotional for single women waiting for the right husband. Each day briefly touches upon a specific spiritual or practical discipline that leads to developing a close relationship with God. Why 31 days? Because it has been said that when we do something for 30 days, it becomes a habit. Therefore, Day 31 represents the first day of your new habit of cultivating a relationship with God by exercising spiritual and practical disciplines on a daily basis.

Every one of us has dreams and desires, and some have thankfully come to fruition. One dream in particular, getting married, occasionally appears to be nowhere in sight, or it was right at our fingertips and was quickly snatched away. Neither are necessarily signs that we will not be blessed with a God-knowing, committed, fun-loving, supportive husband. It only means that the right husband, the man that God has designed, molded, and shaped especially for us, has not arrived yet. So as single women (never married, divorced, or widowed) who want a healthy marriage, we have to patiently wait until it's the right time to enter the world of marriage.

I know that having to wait for anything these days is uncharacteristic of the technological age we are living in. We can:

- email instead of using the post office;
- send a text instead of emailing;
- post an S.O.S. online and quickly receive some kind of feedback.

Communication is sent and received within nano-seconds, and there is little to no waiting involved. But in God's kingdom, we are cautioned to wait for the desires of our hearts and trust God to WOW us.

While waiting can be an arduous process, it is a critical piece to developing a relationship with God. When we wait, we say to Him, "I believe you." When we get ahead of Him, we say, "I don't trust you." Hebrews 11:6 tells us, "And without faith it's impossible to please God, for whoever would approach Him must believe that He exists and that He rewards those who seek Him." It's in the waiting process that we demonstrate faith in God's ability to come through for us in a wonderful way.

God wants us to have our hearts' desires. If it's a marriage that we want, then our Provider wants us to have the very best marriage possible. After all, marriage is a ministry that is supposed to represent the love that God has for us – a love that is true, faithful, unselfish, unconditional, forgiving, merciful, gracious, and compassionate. For that reason, anyone less than God's best will not complement us or resemble God's love.

God showed me through my own singleness how important it is to wait for His blessings and not seek out, hand-pick, and design my husband. I've jump-started some relationships, ignored God's warnings, stuck to my own plan, and played with fire only to end up surrendering to God's will and waiting anyway. By waiting, I have established a wonderful and meaningful relationship with God, and changed the way that I think and make decisions. I can identify and walk away from men who simply are not for me – good men and otherwise – with ease and without regret.

Well, how do we wait? The definition of "wait," according to the Webster's New World Dictionary, is "to stay in place or remain in readiness or in anticipation (until something expected happens or for someone to arrive or catch up)." In other words, we wait by intentionally living every single day with purpose and anticipating that God's very best will show up at the appointed time.

We also wait by developing a profound relationship with God and living firmly in His Word and way. This is accomplished through practicing spiritual and practical disciplines on a daily basis. Both types of disciplines are activities that draw us closer to God and strengthen our spiritual, mental, and emotional muscles and senses, and develop our inner woman. Some examples include reading the Bible and meditating on God's Word, engaging in "me" time and de-cluttering. All that is required is time, space, and the willingness to devote time to God and to make necessary adjustments to our lives.

WHO IS THIS DEVOTIONAL FOR?

This devotional is for:

- all single women who are twiddling their thumbs while waiting for a husband

- all single women who are in need of something purposeful to do while waiting for a husband

- Christian single women who need a new or refresher course on how to develop and maintain a close relationship with God

- Non-Christian single women who are in search of God and a husband

- Non-Christian single women who want to try something new to achieve new and better results

- all women who desire to live a purposeful life

- book clubs and singles ministries

- the curious

INSTRUCTIONS

The waiting room is fully equipped with spiritual and practical disciplines to keep and guide you while waiting for God to send the right husband your way.

For the next 31 days, commit at least 30 minutes a day to proactively draw closer to God. You will need any version of the Holy Bible, a journal and pen, and a dictionary. There are short activities at the end of each devotion to be immediately engaged. These devotions are designed to teach you about spiritual and practical disciplines intended to lead you to the true art of living purposefully. Each one will assist you in cultivating your relationship with God and to help you make necessary changes to your personal life.

DAY 1

Praying: Part 1

...pray without ceasing (1 Thessalonians 5:17 NRSV)

Prayer is the fundamental building block to establishing and maintaining a deep and intimate relationship with God. It's the primary form of communication available to us to remain in contact with the Lord. I must say that prayer is a humbling act, as it guides us to acknowledge the Source of life and leads us to a realization that we are unable to live fulfilling lives without God.

As we pray, there is an exchange of information that takes place between God and us. The more we talk with God, the more our heavenly Father gradually reveals Himself to us. God is relational and prides Himself on being personal and interactive with each of His children. God wants us to know Him and trust in His abilities. And God wants our full attention, especially while we are single and in the waiting room.

Our prayers should be rich with sincerity, boldness, purpose, humility, expectancy, and power. When we meet God in prayer, there should be an expectation that He will hear and answer our prayers. And guess what? He, too, is waiting. God is lovingly and patiently waiting for us to come to Him with our cares, worries, desires, dreams, aspirations, and needs. Our Helper has the solution to all of our life issues.

God wants to hear our melodic voices and desperate cries. He longs for a warm embrace from our spirits. The more we pray, the more our spirits become wrapped up and intertwined with His spirit. This is intimacy at its core.

Prayer is extremely important, and today's scripture urges us to never stop praying. What does this mean? It means that we are to pray when we rise in the morning; are in need of a miracle; have good or poor health; are happy or sad, thankful or ungrateful, in or out of sin, confused or focused, financially fit or financially anemic, famous or unfamiliar; and when we go to bed at night. We should pray for friends, family members, co-workers, strangers, enemies. We should pray about world affairs. Prayer gives us strength, peace, and patience while we wait in the waiting room. It's powerful, and it supernaturally changes people and situations.

How should we pray? While there are a few models of prayer, my suggestion is to simply talk with God. Begin with "Hi, Lord," "Dear God," or whatever you are comfortable with as a form of respect. This is just like addressing someone by name; we should acknowledge Him first. Don't worry about incorporating scriptures into your prayer, unless of course you have this skill. Don't worry about using eloquent words; just be yourself. Don't worry about whether you should close your eyes or not, get on bended knees or not. Prayer can be done while walking, standing, kneeling, bowing, sitting, driving, and even during household chores.

My prayers are not fancy, poetic, or filled with a lot of Christian clichés. In fact, I'm usually all over the place with my prayers until I mentally organize my thoughts and a rhythm develops. But I know that God hears me and answers me regardless of my style — or lack thereof.

Prayer should not be rigid but flexible enough so that we *want* to pray and *enjoy* it. Our hearts are what really matter to God and not our vocabularies, oratory skills, and postures.

Today, as we sit in the waiting room, let's begin making prayer an enjoyable lifestyle.

Activities:

1. Pray now and tell God everything that is on your mind, including your desire for a husband. Be sincere, and don't worry about your style; just talk to him. Include in your prayer a request for God to help make prayer an enjoyable lifestyle.

2. Promise to pray at least twice a day during and after this 31-day journey: once when you get up in the morning and again before you go to bed at night.

3. How about making a request for your husband to be a praying man of God?

DAY 2

Journaling

Thus says the Lord, the God of Israel: Write in a book all the words that I have spoken to you. (Jeremiah 30:2 NRSV)

Journaling is a powerful self-reflective tool and means of communicating with God. Through journaling, we record our deepest feelings, thoughts, regrets, secrets, revelations, dreams, aspirations, prayers, sins, successes, failures, mistakes, needs, and desires, as well as God's instructions. As we express ourselves in written form, a sense of release takes place, and we are encouraged to live the next day with freedom.

Journaling can take on any form: a chronicle of our day, free writing, recording our prayers and the answers to our prayers, poetry, or song. This tool can be used to converse with God and tell Him how much we miss having a decent man in our lives and to express our desire for a husband. We can pour out our hearts to God, telling Him how much we want someone to share our lives with, to grow old with, to attend church with, to have children with — someone to be home when we arrive or to be supportive when we are ill or grieving the loss of a loved one. Then we can record God's response if any.

Journaling is a form of expression that we can grow to love and engage in daily. It's a process that we will at times embrace and at other times reject. There are days when I make only a three-line entry in my journal, and then there are days when I cover at least ten pages a session pertaining to issues on my job or within my family, challenges with a project, health issues, my heart's desires, and so on. Still, there are days when I should journal but do not want to journal and like a disobedient child, won't journal.

This spiritual and practical discipline is liberating. Anything weighing us down will be shed word by word. Petty issues disappear; past hurts are addressed; baggage from previous relationships is destroyed; unforgiveness is brought to the surface and atoned; broken hearts are mended and restored; hidden sins are revealed, and we are able to confess, repent, and give life a fresh start. Journaling while in the waiting room brings about spiritual and inner healing.

This is exciting news especially for those of us who have a tendency to bring unresolved issues into new relationships. Yes, there are some of us who intentionally or unintentionally make our new mates pay for the past mistakes of others. And because of those past mistakes, we come up with unrealistic rules and regulations to govern our relationship that our new mate will eventually fall short of. It's okay to admit it because we can be freed of this behavior right here in the waiting room.

Today, we are encouraged to make journaling a life-style. It reminds us of where we used to be and reveals the path that we are presently on. Journaling may also leave drops of breadcrumbs leading to our futures. The one thing I enjoy the most about journaling is being able to revisit my journals. This is something that I do every year on my birthday because I get to see a pattern of growth that I wouldn't otherwise notice.

Journaling keeps us connected to God and leads us to living freely, peacefully, and joyfully. Begin journaling today.

Activities:

1. If you do not already journal, pen a prayer asking God to help you make journaling a part of your daily life.

2. Practice journaling now by honestly answering the following:

   - Why do you want to get married?
     - o Is it because you were raised in a two-parent household and you want the same type of family structure?
     - o Is it because you were raised in a single-

parent household and you want to build upon a different type of family structure?

- ○ Is it so that you can have a fairytale or your dream wedding?
- ○ Could it be that you do not want to grow old alone?
- ○ Do you want to have a lifelong successful partnership rooted in God?

3. Continue journaling by answering the next set of questions:

- How do you generally feel about not being married yet?
  - ○ Are you angry with God, yourself or with an ex-fiancé? Or are you content, or just merely existing?
- What kind of husband are you waiting for?
- Do you think you've met him already?

DAY 3

Intercessory Prayer

Pray hard and long. Pray for your brothers and sisters. Keep your eyes open. Keep each other's spirits up so that no one falls behind or drops out. (Ephesians 6:18 The Message Bible)

Intercessory prayer is a type of prayer, which in my opinion, is one of the most unselfish acts we as single women can engage in. According to the *Holman Bible Dictionary*, "Intercession is the act of praying to God on behalf of another person." Each of us in the waiting room can give of ourselves by being concerned about one another and lifting each other up in prayer.

The world is saturated with major issues that can be amazingly turned around through intercession, such as:

- high unemployment rate
- failing educational systems
- young children joining gangs
- friends being diagnosed with debilitating or life threatening diseases
- elderly being disrespected and forgotten

These are some of the issues that we as intercessors can pray about. All of us in the waiting room are able to stand in the gap and talk to our heavenly Father on behalf of those in need of drastic change.

Because of intercession, events can miraculously shift in the atmosphere. When God feels and hears our spirits crying out to Him on behalf of others, He responds by calling order, healing, deliverance, protection, encouragement, provision, righteousness, restoration, and holiness into the lives of His children. Whatever is needed, our Provider delivers in abundance.

The closer we get to God, the more our Creator shares His needs and heart's desires with us, His prayer warriors. God relies on us to be obedient to the urges the Holy Spirit deposits into our spirits to pray for others.

Some years ago, there was a period of time when I was waking up almost every morning at 2:00 a.m., and I did not know why. I shared this with a friend, who told me that I needed to pray the next time it happened. So the next time I had a 2:00 a.m. wake-up call from the Holy Spirit, I started praying without knowing what to pray about. But then the Holy Spirit stepped in and guided me to pray for my mentor, who was ill at that time. It became the norm for me to intercede for her whenever I woke up in the wee hours of the morning, and I am glad that I was able to be one of many people who prayed for her healing.

Interceding is a never-ending assignment. Once we end praying for a person, group of people, or set of circumstances, God will send a new assignment our way.

The scripture quoted at the beginning of this devotion tells us to keep our eyes open. In other words, be physically watchful and spiritually attuned to the state of being of others while in the waiting room. As we remain in God, our spirits become sensitive enough to recognize when He speaks and calls us into intercession. Let's be watchful.

Activities:

1. Think about your circle of friends, family members near and far, enemies, co-workers, church family, sorority sisters, and so on.

2. Journal and create a prayer list by writing their names along with their respective situations.

3. Include each person and situation in your prayers daily.

4. Allow God to guide you in your prayers. There may be some people He wants you to spend more time praying for than others. God may also lead you to pray for someone or people who are not on your prayer list, which is fine. Follow the Lord's direction; I'm only providing you with a starting place.

DAY 4

Bible Reading

And the Word became flesh and lived among us, and we have seen his glory, the glory as of a father's only son, full of grace and truth. (John 1:14 NRSV)

The Bible is a love story depicting God's love for humanity. It summarizes God's many attempts to lead the Israelites into a covenant relationship with Him. God forgives them over and over of their adulterous relations with idols or man-made gods. Ultimately he showed humanity what real love is by sacrificing His only begotten Son – Jesus. Sounds like a best seller, huh?

Figuring out where to begin reading the Bible for the first or tenth time is a daunting task. The Bible is made up of 66 books that are divided into the Old and New Testaments. The stories that are knitted together from the first book to the last one are filled with people just like us. Intelligent people. Victorious people. Sinful people. Repentant people. Sick people. Lost people. Purposeful people. Determined people. Believing people. **Waiting people**.

I was taught that the Gospels – Matthew, Mark,

Luke, and John – are the best books to begin reading. Why? The Bible is all about Jesus. While the Old Testament gives an account of Jesus' lineage, the New Testament is about Jesus' ministry on earth. Each Gospel depicts His character differently. In Matthew, Jesus is King; Mark, Jesus is Servant; Luke, Jesus is the Son of Man; and John, Jesus is God.

In reading the Bible and taking in God's truth, the Holy Spirit reshapes of our minds and characters. The more we learn about Jesus, the more we recognize Him as our example of living righteously. We become more loving, positive, patient, disciplined, honest, humble, understanding, merciful, faithful, and comforting women.

Reading God's Word, especially while we are in the waiting room, gives us a change of mind about who we are and how to live as single women. God's Word is meaningful, and it adds value to our lives. It's filled with both spiritual and practical life lessons that we can use daily to effect change and cause transformation to occur. The Bible helps us to see ourselves as God does – His children whom he loves with an everlasting love.

What I love most about reading the Bible is that no matter how many times I read certain passages or stories, something new stands out to me. God's Word is always fresh, and I am encouraged by it. The Bible renews my understanding of life and who God is to me. God's Word gives me a sense of peace and puts me at ease whenever I am worried, anxious, lonely, sad, or depressed. His Word is satisfying to my soul and it pleases the soul of anyone who reads it for truth, understanding, and wisdom. Get to know God better by reading His Word daily.

Activities:

1. Pray and ask God to help you clear your calendar of every unnecessary activity so that you can devote time to reading His Word daily.

2. Start reading the Word today with the book of Matthew. Jot down in your journal the beginning and ending verses so that you can keep track of your progress.

3. List any verses that you have difficulty understanding or believing.

4. Pray again and ask God to increase your faith in Him and to remove any and all doubt that His Son Jesus walked this earth.

DAY 5

Biblical Meditation

Mine eyes prevent the night watches, that I might meditate in thy word. (Psalms 119:148 KJV)

Biblical meditation is reading the Word and then reflecting upon it. When meditating on God's Word, we are turning it over and over in our minds until we reach an understanding of what the Word means to us and how it applies to our lives.

The process of biblical meditation is equal to that of mulling over a bad breakup. We replay events, scenes, conversations, and the like repeatedly. We think back to and obsess over when we and how we said "a,b,c" and then how he over reacted when he did "x,y,z." Much time is spent on breaking down big issues into small pieces to arrive at the essence of the breakup. Biblical meditation dissects big issues into manageable parts and gives us insights pertaining to our lives so that we can make sound decisions and necessary changes.

This spiritual discipline doesn't entail emptying ourselves and disconnecting from reality. In fact, the opposite occurs. We are in the moment and the

Holy Spirit leads us to acknowledge that we are alive because of God. A sense of peace sweeps over us – which is the state of being we strive for – and we can acknowledge that our existence is solely due to God's grace and mercy.

Through biblical meditation, God pours out His love for us by speaking to specific situations in our lives – unemployment, falling businesses, health issues, wayward children, impending danger, broken hearts, longing hearts, or hidden sins – to heal, deliver, protect, love, and transform us. This spiritual discipline brings restoration to our souls and gives us a sense of knowing God on a higher level. When we intentionally pursue God and develop a deep relationship with Him, our experience with God is different every time we meet with Him in the waiting room.

Creating an environment that is conducive to meditating is important to the effectiveness of biblical meditation. There are several ways to meditate, but I have created the STAR Method as a guide to assist with regularly engaging biblical meditation.

Tools: Bible, dictionary, journal, time, and a quiet space.

The STAR Method:

Scripture – Pray and ask God to lead you to the passage of scripture He wants to use to communicate with you.

Think – Read and write out the scripture in your journal. Think deeply about it; turn it over in your mind several times. Consider each word, and look up the meaning of any words that are unfamiliar to you. This will highlight the richness of the text.

Apply – Ask yourself some thought-provoking questions, such as: Why did God lead me to this scripture? Is God pointing out a specific character flaw? What sins have I not confessed? Is God encouraging me? Is God telling me to trust Him and not be afraid? Is God promising me something or reminding me of one of His promises? Journal what the passage is saying to you and then write out a plan for applying it to your life.

Repeat – We learn by repetition. Continue practicing biblical meditation using the STAR Method, while in the waiting room, until it becomes second nature.

Activities:

1. Pray and ask God to help you cultivate a lifestyle of meditating biblically.

2. Practice the STAR Method to meditate. (Either ask God to lead you to a scripture, or begin with Psalms 23:1-3.)

DAY 6

Memorizing Scripture

I treasure your word in my heart, so that I may not sin against you. (Psalms 119:11 NRSV)

Memorizing scripture goes together with reading and meditating on the Word. The more we engage these two spiritual disciplines together, the more we expose ourselves to scriptures that resonate with us. These are the verses that tend to be easy to memorize because they speak to familiar places in our lives.

There are benefits to memorizing scripture. As indicated in the scripture quoted at the beginning of this devotion, knowing the Word prevents us from sinning. Many of us are familiar with the saying "when you know better, you do better." The same concept applies to memorizing God's Word. When we know it, the Word becomes that much more difficult to stray from it.

God's Word is a weapon of warfare. There is good and evil in this world, and life is not absent of spiritual battles. Satan will tempt, trick, deceive, worry, confuse, and wreak havoc in our lives while we are in the waiting room. By speaking God's Word to our battles – drama on the job, sickness in our bodies, family issues, depression, temptation – a divine shield surrounds us, protects us, and keeps us from falling.

The Word encourages us during those times when we see seemingly happily married couples walking together, having a date night, being publicly affectionate, attending church or other functions together. When we are reminded that we are not married yet and are feeling low and lonely, being able to recite God's Word can and will refresh and revive us. His Word is full of promise, and we can depend on it at all times to restore and resuscitate our lives.

I recall becoming discouraged while writing this book. Feelings of doubt and fear rose up in me. And then I remembered God's Word, "I am about to do a new thing; now it springs forth, do you not perceive it?" This is Isaiah 43:19, and it's one of God's promises to me (and to you too). It helped me complete this devotional and reminded me that God has great things in store for me (and you too).

Let's treasure God's Word in our hearts.

Activities:

1. Pray and ask God to help you make memorizing scripture part of your Bible study. As soon as you come across a scripture that speaks to you, jot it down on several index cards. Sometimes writing scripture repeatedly helps with

memorizing it.

2. You may want to record yourself reading the verse that speaks to you. Play it back and listen to your recording as you walk, clean, exercise, drive, and so on.

3. Strategically post your index cards in places within your home that you frequently visit; e.g., the bathroom mirror, the refrigerator, and your bedroom nightstand. If possible, post them around your desk at work.

4. Test yourself by saying the verse without looking at the index card. Incorporate it into your prayers, and ask someone to test you.

5. Begin with today's scripture.

DAY 7

Praying God's Word

...he sent out his word and healed them, and delivered them from destruction. (Psalms 107:20 NRSV)

Praying God's Word demonstrates our relationship with Him and our knowledge of the Word. This spiritual discipline affirms that we believe and have faith in God's ability to inexplicably come through for us. God's Word provides substance for our prayers and keeps us attuned to the One who not only hears our prayers but answers them right on time.

In order to pray God's Word, we have to know it. We learn the Word by reading the Bible, memorizing scriptures, meditating, and journaling. As we engage these spiritual disciplines, God's Word takes root in our spirits, lives in our mouths, and is hidden on our hearts. Consequently, this equips us with the ability to pray God's Word back to Him with confidence and hope.

Today's scripture tells us that people were healed and delivered by God's Word. We can be, too, while sitting in the waiting room. God's Word is powerful, phenomenal, and authoritative. His

Word is effective and is appropriate for every situation because it's the truth.

Have you ever heard people say, "My word is my bound?" What this means is that there is a guarantee attached to their word. The same holds true with the Word of God; His Word is saturated with promises that will be realized in time.

The Bible tells us that God watches over His Word to perform it in our lives (Jeremiah 1:12). Whatever God has promised us; He will bring it to fruition. If God promised healing, then we are as good as healed. If God promised a new job, praise Him until and long after the official acceptance letter is signed. If God promised a husband, wait for His best and do not settle for someone to temporarily take the sting out of being single.

We will know God's best by some of the following:

- his core values
- his level of integrity and authenticity
- his relationship with God
- the decency of his actions
- the quality of his conversation

This is not by any means an exhaustive list of what to look for in a husband. In order to recognize God's best, we have to remain close to God because He will reveal that person to us in due time.

Begin using God's Word in prayer today and notice how much more powerful your prayers become.

Activities:

1. Sit in silence for 10 minutes.

2. Practice incorporating one of the following scriptures into your prayers as it applies to you:

   a. Forgiveness: 1 John 1:9

   b. Healing: Psalms 103:3

   c. Love: Jeremiah 31:3

   d. Temptation: 1 Corinthians 10:13

   e. Peace: Isaiah 26:12

   f. Loneliness: John 14:1

3. You may want to begin your prayers by saying, "God, your Word tells me..." or "God, your Word promises..."

4. Memorize the scripture you used in this prayer (and hide it in your heart).

5. Praise God for teaching you His Word to pray back to Him.

6. Practice, practice, and practice.

DAY 8

Prayer Partner

First of all, then, I urge that supplications, prayers, intercessions, and thanksgivings be made for everyone, for kings and all who are in high positions, so that we may lead a quiet and peaceable life in all godliness and dignity. This is right and is acceptable in the sight of God our Savior, who desires everyone to be saved and to come to the knowledge of the truth. (1 Timothy 2:1-4 NRSV)

Having a prayer partner is a beautiful experience. Together, praying, praising, interceding, and lifting up thanksgiving to God is a powerful practice. The Bible tells us that when two or more are gathered in His name, He is in their midst (Matthew 18:20). In other words, numbers equal strength.

A prayer partner is someone we meet with on a regular basis to pray about any matter together. Prayer partners lift up prayers that can miraculously change world affairs, issues on our jobs, sickness in our bodies, generational curses, disorder in our homes, church growth, and desires to amend estranged relationships. Anything and everything can be touched upon during prayer sessions.

Praying with a partner may very well feel awkward

initially, and it can be intimidating. Each of us has a particular style, and many of us have not found our own voice in prayer yet, which is fine. We may be made nervous by those we deem professional prayer warriors. But all that matters is that we know God, and have a sincere heart and a desire for a miraculous change to take place.

It's important for us to bring everything to God, including asking Him to lead us to a prayer partner. He will match us up with someone whom we can trust, mature with, learn from, and be vulnerable with. It's a powerful and life-changing journey for as long as the two touch and agree.

While you're praying, pay attention to the rhythm that develops. There will be short pauses and periods of silence. Don't rush! Allow God to use this space to speak, heal, love on both of you, redirect your prayers, and so forth. Weeping or crying may occur. Don't be nervous or afraid. This is an indication of God's cleansing or the outpouring of His love. Whatever is happening, just be in the moment.

Lastly, prayer partners can meet in person at various venues to pray. This is the fun part, because we can be as creative and as free as possible. Sessions are not limited to one specific place. Pray in parks or gardens, on street corners, in churches, in each other's homes, or via telephone or video conference. Prayer partners can pray anywhere together, including in the waiting room, as long as it's done in Jesus' name.

Activities:

1. If you do not already have a prayer partner, ask God to lead you to someone with whom you will be compatible. If you have a prayer partner and it's not working out, ask God to help you to amicably end that relationship and lead you to the right prayer partner.

2. When that person presents herself to you, spend some time talking and sharing a little about yourselves to break the ice (even if you are somewhat familiar with each other).

3. Come up with a schedule to pray. You might be a morning person, and she might be a night person. This will be challenging at first, but it can and will work out.

4. Create a list of prayer concerns and associated scriptures. This will help to guide your prayers when you get started. Once the two of you become comfortable, more experienced, and familiar with your rhythm as a team, the list will become unnecessary.

5. The two of you may want to keep a prayer journal to track your prayers and when and how God answered them. *(You may also want to fast together to complement your prayer sessions. More on fasting to come.)*

DAY 9

Practicing Silence

But oh! God is in his holy Temple! Quiet everyone – a holy silence. Listen! (Habakkuk 2:20 The Message)

Shhhhh…God is commanding silence right now. We have been busy all day and all week, and God wants us to sit in silence and commune with Him.

Practicing silence requires us to isolate ourselves from our normal activity-filled environments for the purpose of reverencing God and listening for Him. This means no sounds. No music or TV. No people. No busyness. No gadgets. No worries. No plans. Only God and us silently communicating with each other in the waiting room.

Silence is an amazing experience. It opens our spirits up to God to feed off His wholesome presence. It's in silence that His presence is pronounced and surreal. God sits and dines with us, and makes remarkable deposits into our spirits. We become satisfied because of God's generosity and elated by His joy. There is a level of communication that takes place in silence between God and us that cannot be compared to any experience on earth.

This spiritual discipline teaches us how to recognize God's voice. The more time we spend alone with God in silence, the easier it becomes to identify God's voice even in the midst of distractions. It's in silence that God gives us revelatory knowledge and blesses us with "a-ha!" moments. He reminds us how much He loves us and gives us glimpses of our futures.

When practicing silence, our thoughts will certainly compete with the stillness of the atmosphere and try to distract us. Our desires for a husband may begin to play out in our minds. We may begin to imagine what he looks like. Is he tall or short? Skinny or heavy? Bald head or long locs? What kind of job does he have? Has he been married before? Does he get along with his parents? Is the man I'm dating my husband? I've been divorced for a while. Will I re-marry? I've been a widow far too long. Is there someone else for me? When this happens, immediately say to your mind, "STOP," and toss those thoughts out. This is not the space to be thinking about these matters. The discipline of silence is a time of worship, and it takes time to develop.

I used to think about everything under the sun when I initially started practicing silence. I would be in complete stillness, and just when I set out to focus on God, thoughts about my bills, student loans, job, someone on the train, cleaning my house, putting gas in my car, taking a vacation, getting married, and so on would pop into my mind. I would shake my head and say, "STOP," in order to center myself and focus on God.

While sitting in the waiting room, let's get to know God through silence. He is waiting to sit with us in the stillness of the moment and share His wonders, peace, and love with each of us.

Activities:

1. Practice silence for 10 minutes daily. Make sure you have your journal with you.

2. Sit and close your eyes. Take two to three minutes to quiet your mind and release all distracting thoughts.

3. Ask God to speak to you.

4. Don't pray; just listen for the sweet nothings that He may whisper into your spirit.

5. Record what He says to you.

6. Don't worry if you don't hear from God right away. This takes time and practice. Continue tomorrow.

DAY 10

Taming The Tongue

…but no one can tame the tongue – a restless evil, full of deadly poison. With it we bless the Lord and Father, and with it we curse those who are made in the likeness of God. From the same mouth come blessing and cursing. My brothers and sisters, this ought not to be so. (James 3:8-10 NRSV)

The Bible tells us something very interesting …animals have been (and still are) tamed by humans. But no one can tame the human tongue. Whoa!

The tongue, the fleshy organ that houses our taste buds is the most dangerous part of our bodies. My mother used to say, "Watch your mouth," which is the same as "Tame your tongue." Through our tongues we have cursed out and disrespected folk, destroyed reputations, ruined relationships, reduced people's self-esteem, snuffed out dreams, nullified plans, and spiritually killed people. The ability to destroy all that is lovely, beautiful, possible, creative, intelligent, and special is in our mouths.

It's my belief that the ego and lack of self-control are at the core of our destructive tongues. We have to: be right, hurt the worst, get revenge, be on top, be real, be smarter, be the best, be number one, be first, have the last word; we have to win. Meanwhile, the most important relationship we have is being destroyed – our relationship with God. Every time ugly words flow out of our mouths, a cancer develops within us and begins to eat away at our connection to God.

God doesn't deal with or appreciate arrogance on any level. In fact, God "opposes the proud but gives grace to the humble" (James 4:6). So while we are in the waiting room, let's ask Jesus to show us how to humble ourselves and help us to exercise self-control. These two virtues will come in handy when we are no longer in the waiting room.

When we are married, there will be times of disagreements and arguments. Humility and self-control will have to kick in just so we do not curse the man that's made in God's likeness. If not, we will create distance in our homes and also between God and us and end up losing instead of winning.

It's important to seek Jesus' help now to refrain from using our tongues as weapons of mass destruction, especially since we will be held accountable for every careless word that we speak (Matthew 12:36).

Activities:

1. Sit in silence for 10 minutes.

2. Jot down in your journal the last time you said

something that brought harm to someone. What was the situation, and what happened?

3. Be bold. If you haven't apologized to that person, do so right away.

4. Pray and ask God to forgive you for sinning in thought, word, and deed (remember, our thoughts develop into words and then into actions).

5. Also ask God to remove your ego and replenish your spirit with humility so that you are not quick to speak harshly and subsequently destroy other people.

6. Meditate on James 1:19 and journal what it means to you.

DAY 11

Practicing Praise

I call upon the Lord, who is worthy to be praised, so I shall be saved from my enemies. (Psalms 18:3 NRSV)

Praise is both a spiritual discipline and a warfare tool. It's a powerful act of worship that releases God's power into the atmosphere when our enemies –Satan and his minions – are riding our backs and weighing us down. Praise says to God, "I need the only One who is able to save me from this situation NOW!"

Every now and then we are tempted by our own natural desires and certainly by Satan. He is serious about his goal to destroy all those who are actively pursuing God and living righteously.

Satan is cunning and sneaky. He will quickly slither into any situation where vulnerability, loneliness, or desperation is present and try to tear us down. He will bombard our minds with any of the following thoughts:

- alcohol cravings
- an ex from way back when
- cigarette hungers

- doubt and fear
- feelings of lust
- feelings of loneliness and despair
- feelings of being ugly and unattractive
- food cravings or emotional shopping
- negative or suicidal thoughts
- thoughts of not being good enough
- feelings of being unworthy of God's love

On the surface it may not seem like it, but these are emergency situations that require praise on the spot. Don't delay! When Satan dispatches his minions to us, it's serious business. This is a sign that we are doing something right in the waiting room as it relates to our relationship with God.

Satan doesn't want us to successfully wait for God. He would love for us to:

- eat until diabetes, high blood pressure and obesity settles in
- go against our morals and values
- jump from one bad relationship to another
- sleep with every Michael, Joe and Rick
- shop until we are in debt
- take our lives

Satan is out to destroy us, and he is relentless. Therefore, we must be more serious than he is and stop whatever we're doing; open up our mouths and acknowledge God's awesomeness and power when the pressures of life are too overbearing.

That's right! Let's do as the psalmist says: "Call upon God who is praise-worthy." Exalt God. Extol God. Bless God. Glorify God. Magnify God. In other words, tell Him that He is great, excellent, wonderful, tremendous, awesome, lovely, all of that. Tell Him that He is your keeper, portion, strength, friend, deliverer, protector, and all that you need. Satan and his subordinates will promptly flee, as they cannot effectively operate in an atmosphere of praise because God shows up.

Praise, just like the other spiritual disciplines, takes practice. Let's not wait until we are being tempted, in warfare, or having moments of loneliness to praise God. Let's start practicing praising God while we are in the waiting room in order to build up our praise muscles and endurance.

Activities:

1. Sit in silence for ten minutes.

2. Research the many attributes of God; e.g., He's the creator of heaven and earth, a provider, a healer, and a deliverer.

3. Write out the scripture references that describe His character and memorize at least three.

4. Practice reciting aloud God's attributes – practice praise.

5. Pray and ask God to show you who He has been to you lately, and journal whatever God reveals to you.

DAY 12

Being Teachable

Listen to advice and accept instruction, that you may gain wisdom for the future. (Proverbs 19:20 NRSV)

Being teachable is the willingness to listen to, receive, and apply sound advice from others. In order to be teachable, we must possess and demonstrate humility, meaning that we have to recognize and acknowledge that we simply do not know everything.

People with teachable spirits willingly sit at the feet of knowledgeable and wise folk and soak up all that they have to share. They take copious mental and physical notes and immediately envision how and when they will apply their new understanding.

As we sit in the waiting room, this is the ideal time to develop a humble spirit and become teachable. Scattered throughout our lives are couples who have been married for 15, 20, 30, or even 40-plus years who undoubtedly experienced all kind of life and relationship issues. I am not discounting the good times, but it's the unfortunate, challenging, and difficult times that we can learn from.

Long-term married couples have experienced:

- disappointments and forgiveness
- leaving and returning
- wanting to leave but remaining and enduring
- stints of insecurities and loneliness
- days of regrets
- stages of sickness
- periods of being discontent
- times of financial distress

Any type of hardship, difficult season, or emotional roller-coaster ride that can be experienced, long-term married couples most likely have been through it and have survived. **WE NEED TO TALK WITH THEM.**

While in the waiting room, this is the time for us to seek free and valuable counsel. Our assignment as students is to talk with as many long-term married couples as possible to find out what sustained them during the hard times. It's easy to love and be happy during the jubilant seasons. But when the challenges come, will we fold, or will we stand firmly, endure and come out victoriously?

Activities:

1. Pray and ask God to give you a teachable spirit. Ask Him to remove all logical thinking, arrogance, and ego and replenish you with humility.

2. Diligently search out a few long-term married couples in your family, friends, church, sorority,

professional organizations, job, neighborhood, and so on, and engage them in conversation about how they are maintaining their marriage. Ask specific and hard questions.

3. Make it a habit to periodically sit at their feet and take in all of the advice that they offer.

4. Maintain a separate journal to refer back to these conversations when necessary.

5. Be proactive and begin praying now for God to give you and your husband-to-be the strength, wisdom, and capacity to maintain a healthy marriage.

DAY 13

Accountability Partner

My friends, if anyone is detected in a transgression, you who have received the Spirit should restore such a one in a spirit of gentleness. Take care that you yourselves are not tempted. Bear one another's burdens, and in this way you will fulfill the law of Christ. (Galatians 6:1 – 2 NRSV)

Someone once said that old habits are hard to break, and I agree. I also believe that new and healthy behaviors are difficult to begin and cultivate. That is why having an accountability partner is key to our growth as individuals.

An accountability partner is someone whom we trust and respect to assist us with making righteous decisions, overcoming temptations, and reaching specific goals. This person is tough and yet gentle. She is not going to tell us what we want to hear, support our poor choices, or allow us to sell out or quit. However, she will be honest when we are going astray and gently redirect our focus back to Jesus and to our personal and spiritual goals.

We are not perfect. The Word clearly tells us that we fall short of the glory of God every day (Romans 3:23). And at times we truly need the help of someone else to get back on track.

God always knows what we need long before we realize it. For example, God sacrificed His son at Calvary light-years before we were born. He knew then what we would need today: a Savior, healer, deliverer, and divine friend. God also knew that sitting in this waiting room would become difficult at some point for each of us. Therefore, He provided us with a tool to aid us in our waiting: an accountability partner.

Remember that prayer is appropriate for all things, even when in search of an accountability partner. Just as in a marriage, only the right person can effectively serve in this capacity. Our accountability partners have to be willing to do the hard work of checking, motivating, and redirecting us back to the new and healthy habits we are developing.

Once an accountability partner has been chosen, we have to make a conscious decision to open our personal space to that person. Because this person will not be with us every second of the day, she will call, text, or send emails asking questions to gauge our progress and to encourage us when we fall short.

So, which of the following bad habits do you need assistance with giving up in order today to live a healthy and fulfilling life?

- Excessive shopping
- Drinking

- Fornicating
- Gossiping
- Lying
- Manipulating
- Over-eating
- Procrastinating
- Smoking
- Stealing
- Something else

What personal and spiritual goals would you like to achieve?

- Acquiring a new skill
- Arriving at work or for appointments on time
- Becoming an entrepreneur
- Changing your career
- Changing your diet
- Completing a degree or certificate program
- Controlling your anger or tongue
- Exercising daily
- Memorizing scripture
- Reading and studying the Word
- Taking the GMAT/GRE
- Writing a book

We are never alone in the waiting room. There are like-minded women amongst us with similar goals and plans who can help us along the way. Be courageous and ask someone today to serve as your accountability partner.

Activities:

1. Think about those individuals whom you truly respect and whom you know will be honest with you.

2. Select a person to serve as your accountability partner.

3. Tell her exactly what you need help with and agree upon the duration of your new relationship.

4. Give her permission to ask personal questions.

5. Establish the best time for your accountability partner to call you, and vice versa. *You may need to reach out to that person if you are on the brink of doing something that you really do not want to do.*

6. Keep a journal of your progress. Start by jotting down your accountability partner's name and contact information, and what you need help with.

7. Keep in mind that there may come a time when your accountability partner will experience some ups and downs, too. It's okay to help her. *To accountability partners: Please do not be judgmental.* Read and memorize Romans 3:23.

8. At the end of your journey together, be sure to say thank you.

DAY 14

Creating Boundaries

For among them are those who make their way into households and captivate silly women, overwhelmed by their sins and swayed by all kinds of desires... (2 Timothy 3:6 NRSV)

Creating boundaries, in general, defines the extent to which we allow people to enter our physical, mental, emotional, and spiritual spaces. It's a form of protection and a way to command respect, especially from men who are courting us, or whom we are dating or maintaining a plutonic relationship with. By creating boundaries we are raising the bar on respect.

Respect is the foundation of all relationships, and setting boundaries helps us to recognize when we are being disrespected, mistreated, or manipulated, or when we are moving too fast in a new relationship. Having absolutely no boundaries gives the wrong message. It says that any and all behavior will be accepted. Remember that, as single, wise women, we have the power to set the pace of a relationship – dating or plutonic.

We do not have to go with the flow. Sometimes the

flow of a relationship leads us to a destination that is not meant for us. At times, we get caught up in the excitement and newness of a relationship and go too far too soon. We skip over holding hands and walking in the park to having a late-night dinner and bringing our date home. Next, we are kissing behind closed doors and then finding ourselves in compromising positions. Boundaries help us to shamelessly save our bodies for our wedding night.

The waiting room is the perfect place to establish boundaries. It's in this space that God is showing us who He created us to be – worshippers of God – how to love and value ourselves, and how to make discerned decisions. As we become the women that God planned for us to be, the importance of setting boundaries will become that much clearer and more desirable to us.

Activities:

1. Pray and ask God to reveal to you every time you've allowed men to violate your space and disrespect you. Journal whatever He reveals to you.

2. Now ask God to deliver you from any and all forms of low self-esteem, self-hatred, desperation, and neediness, and to replenish you with self-love, self-respect, and clearly defined boundaries to establish for yourself.

3. Journal: How many times have you gone with the flow of a relationship and then ended up in

a disaster? Record the details. Moving forward, what will you do differently?

4. Praise God for the power to create boundaries and to start a fresh life.

DAY 15

Saying "No"

Am I now seeking human approval, or God's approval? Or am I trying to please people? If I were still pleasing people, I would not be a servant of Christ. (Galatians 1:10 NRSV)

Are you a people pleaser? Do you suffer from guilt as soon as the desire to tell someone "no" rises up in you? Do you beat up on yourself after saying "yes" to a request or assignment when you should have said "no?" Do you resentfully shuffle appointments around on your calendar and alter your plans to accommodate the request or assignment? If you've answered "yes" to any of the previous questions, know that you are not alone.

Many of us want to demonstrate that we are loyal, dependable, and competent women, and to some extent make people happy as well. But at times we do this to our own detriment by agreeing to requests or accepting assignments, projects, and responsibilities that we do not have time for or the desire to handle. In the meantime, by saying "yes" we've disappointed the only one we have to please: God.

God knows that our "yes" is inauthentic and it was induced by a lack of courage on our part to say "no." We know it, too, and it makes us sick to our stomachs as a consequence, because now we have to carry out a lie with a smile on our face. Our stress level is off the chart because of all the thoughts swarming around in our heads: "I really don't want to do this; I could kick myself." "Why didn't I say no?" "Maybe I can come up with an excuse now to get me out of this commitment." "Now I'm committed so I have to follow through, ughhhh."

It's okay to tell people "no" even if it means having fewer friends, no longer being popular, or disappointing others. There are some responsibilities we do not have to own, events we do not have to chair or attend, favors to give, and so forth.

Today we are challenged with taking a stand to let our "no" be "no" and to live guilt-free. This, too, can be accomplished in the waiting room.

Activities:

1. Begin saying "no" to:

    a. requests that are not in line with who you are

    b. activities that do not coincide with your calendar

    c. people who always suck the life out of you

    d. responsibilities you honestly cannot or do not want to fulfill

e. chairing the next birthday celebration, anniversary, wedding, baby shower, going-away party, and anything you want to say "no" to and be okay with your decision

f. things that bring clutter to your life

2. Journal this experience and indicate how difficult it was to say "no" the first time? Did you feel guilty? Have you lost any friends? Have people become angry with you?

3. Pray and ask God to remove all guilt from you as you begin to say "no" to requests you do not want to honor. Ask Him to prepare the hearts of the requestors to receive your "no" in love and with understanding.

4. Ask God to point out to you anyone who has been taking advantage of your kindness. Have a conversation with that person and gently tell him or her that you can no longer serve him or her in the same capacity.

5. Praise God for the right to say "no" and to live guilt-free.

6. Meditate on and memorize today's scripture.

DAY 16

De-Cluttering

For everything there is a season, and a time for every matter under heaven: a time to seek, and a time to lose; a time to keep, and a time to throw away; (Ecclesiastes 3:1 and 6 NRSV)

The time to take inventory of the clutter in our lives, get rid of it, and make room for newness is upon us. The idea of clutter can be misleading because some of us tend to think that only a clearly disorganized space qualifies as clutter. Not true. Clutter can be neatly tucked away in physical spaces, discreetly hidden in the recesses of our hearts and souls and concealed in our minds.

De-cluttering, or removing clutter, is the process of ridding ourselves of accumulated things, toxic people, and unhealthy ways to create a clear path for communion with God and to live freely. When we are meeting with God, it's essential that we are able to center ourselves to be at one with the Lord. We hinder our ability to tap into those deep places of God when clutter exists in our lives.

Clutter contributes to our inability to function at full capacity because it robs us of our physical, spiritual, emotional, and mental energy. It's challenging for us to think and see things clearly when every time we turn, clutter greets us. It says, "Hello," and we ignore it.

Clutter depletes our energy because we exert too much of it trying to adapt to or ignore clutter. This is not how God intended for us to live while in the waiting room and beyond. We are supposed to freely live, move, and have our being, and not be trapped and hindered by stuff, people, and unhealthy lifestyles.

The following are examples of physical, spiritual, emotional, or mental clutter:

Physical Clutter

- a junky car
- anything that represents the old you
- dead plants
- items with emotional ties
- lingering ex-boyfriends or lovers
- messy pocketbooks and wallets
- negative people
- piles of mail, receipts, magazines, newspapers, greeting cards, and old letters (I recently shredded several letters from an ex from the 1990s; it's 2012.)
- stuff from men from your past
- the closet you dread to open and the proverbial junk drawer

Spiritual Clutter

- addictions
- envy or jealousy
- habitual behaviors
- hatred
- unclean thoughts
- unconfessed sins
- unforgiveness
- unproductive ministries and organizations

Emotional or Mental Clutter

- being disorganized
- chaos
- confusion; inability to think clearly and make sound decisions
- estranged relationships
- family, work, and friend drama
- forgetfulness, being a scatterbrain

Sweep, mop, bag, throw away, and release clutter of every kind. Welcome God into a clutter-free space. Begin to feel the lightness in the atmosphere and His spirit freely flowing everywhere our feet tread.

Activities:

1. Sit in silence for 10 minutes.

2. Meditate on and memorize today's scripture.

3. Pray and ask God to reveal to you all of the clutter that is in your life. Then ask yourself and God whether or not there is room in your life for a husband. If not, what do you need to rid yourself of to fit your husband-to-be in your life?

4. Journal whatever God shares with you. Feel free to use my examples of physical, spiritual, emotional, or mental clutter as a starting point to create your list.

5. Develop an action plan, including a timeline, for your de-cluttering project. Be patient with yourself and the process. Keep in mind that it's easy to create clutter, but it's difficult to get rid of it. This is a long-term project.

DAY 17

Living Simply

"Do not store up for yourselves treasures on earth, where moth and rust consume and where thieves break in and steal; but store up for yourselves treasures in heaven, where neither moth nor rust consumes and where thieves do not break in and steal. For where your treasure is, there your heart will be also. (Matthew 6:19-21 NRSV)

Living simply is focusing on God and knowing that real treasure is with Him. It's also exercising self-control, especially in the area of spending. Being practical consumers of goods and services leads us to purchasing necessary and meaningful belongings. Doing so prevents us from accumulating needless stuff and living beyond our means.

Living simply means that we are not giving in to the pressures of the world and competing with family, friends, co-workers, and next-door neighbors to have the latest and greatest TV, handbag, shoes, car, electronic gadget, and so on. Instead, we understand that material things are fun but do not define or complete us. Things break, disappear, fade away, shrink, and become outdated. But

God's treasure has everlasting life.

Hopefully, de-cluttering will reveal to us that we do not need everything we possess. Things sometimes give us a false sense of self, security, and satisfaction. If we are not careful, we may find ourselves purchasing items and stuffing our closets, drawers, and shelves with pointless bits and pieces to fill a void. Keep in mind that there is absolutely nothing wrong with having material things. But when things become our focus, this is an indication that we are in need of something meaningful and fulfilling in our lives – God.

Some of the benefits of living simply are:

- being able to build a savings account
- being able to help someone in need
- being able to save enough money to purchase a home
- being debt-free
- having less clutter
- living stress-free

Accumulating the fruit of the Spirit is the direction to move in. Who doesn't need an abundance of love, joy, peace, patience, kindness, generosity, faithfulness, gentleness, and self-control? The beauty of the fruit of the Spirit is that it's free.

God's Word tells us that we cannot have too much fruit. (Galatians 5:23) So, while we are in the waiting room, let's build and maintain a productive relationship with God and yield spiritual fruit. We will attract the right people and husband into our lives and hopefully lead others to Christ.

Activities:

1. Continue de-cluttering.

2. Monitor your spending habits for 30 days. Maintain a daily journal of everything you buy.

3. Organize your purchases into categories such as food, clothing, shoes, housewares, jewelry, books, CDs, etc. Tally up how much money was spent in each category.

4. Decide which things are necessities and which are not, and then commit to changing your spending habits.

5. Pray and ask God to help you develop self-control in the area of spending.

6. Ask your prayer partner to add you to the prayer list.

7. Ask your accountability partner for help with living simply.

DAY 18

Temple Care

You realize, don't you, that you are the temple of God, and God himself is present in you? No one will get by with vandalizing God's temple, you can be sure of that. God's temple is sacred – and you, remember, are the temple. (1 Corinthians 3:16 – 17 The Message)

During Old Testament times, temples were sacred places of worship, and not just anything or anyone could enter them. The interior and exterior were beautifully adorned with gold carvings, exquisite jewels, and large statues of angels. King Solomon built a temple for God, and, according to 1 Kings 6:20, the inner sanctuary "was overlaid with pure gold." It had to be absolutely beautiful and clean in order for God to dwell there.

Our bodies are no different. We are the living, breathing, walking, and talking temples of God. The Holy Spirit lives within each of us, and our bodies should be appropriate dwelling places for Him.

Who wants to live in a foul, polluted or diseased-infested home? None of us, and neither does God. The prerequisite for temple care is self-love. When we love ourselves, we understand our worth and treat our bodies with tender, loving care. Treating our bodies casually, irresponsibly, or destructively through bad habits or dangerous social behaviors simply is not an option for God's children.

All foul things are prohibited from entering God's temple. Foul things are anything that can pollute the body and cause disease to attack and eventually destroy it.

Cigarettes, marijuana, ecstasy, cocaine, heroin, inhalant drugs, and the like are prohibited. Excessive alcohol, soda, sugary drinks, and foods...prohibited. Fatty, greasy, salty, fried, late-night-carb, processed foods...prohibited.

Eating properly and exercising regularly can prevent some diseases. Replace poor eating habits and dangerous social behaviors with proper nutrition and fitness. Consume fruits, vegetables, whole grains, legumes, and nuts. These foods reduce our chances of having high blood pressure, high cholesterol, diabetes, poor circulation, fibroids, and uterine cysts.

Eating properly can certainly be boring. I learned this when I changed my diet due to my battles with endometriosis, cysts, and fibroids a few years ago. First I became a vegetarian and then graduated to veganism. Because my meals bored me to tears, I added fish back into my diet. Today, I no longer suffer with debilitating pain from female issues.

Oh, yeah, I take spinning classes, too. Spinning is a

BEAST; it is not for the weak and I refuse to let it conquer me. It is a great cardio workout; try it at your own risk.

While gym memberships can be expensive, it costs nothing to jog, run, power walk, or jump rope in our neighborhoods; stretch; or engage in yoga at home. Any form of exercise that is easy to do in and around the home is beneficial to us. Research the Internet for nutritious meal plans and deals on gym memberships. If you are dealing with alcohol or drug problems, research the Internet for outreach programs that offer services to assist you with changing your lifestyle.

Let's honor God by honoring our bodies while in the waiting room and beyond.

Activities:

1. Sit in silence for 10 minutes.

2. Meditate on today's scripture.

3. Journal a prayer to God. If you have not been taking care of His temple, (your body) confess your neglect and ask for forgiveness.

4. Praise God for your health and wellness.

5. Seek out an accountability partner, if you haven't already, to assist you with changing your lifestyle including diets, exercising, and recreational activities. *Lifestyle changes can be difficult and may require help from other people.*

6. Maintain a lifestyle journal for 30 days. Record everything that you consume and the behaviors you engage in so you can review where changes need to be made.

7. Make necessary changes.

DAY 19

"Me" Time

For everything there is a season, and time for every matter under heaven. (Ecclesiastes 3:1 NRSV)

It's time for some "me" time in the waiting room!

"Me" time sounds a little selfish, and the thought of it stirs up anxiety in some of us. The notion of ceasing to be everything to everyone for a little while and investing time in ourselves appears to be wrong, for some strange reason. Maybe it's because we are women.

It's in our DNA, single or not, to wear many hats, and we do not know when to hang them up even for a little while. We are heads of households, mothers, mentors, caretakers, organizers, peace-makers, chauffeurs, creators, leaders, problem solvers, chefs, doctors, counselors. And guess what? We deserve some "me" time.

A reprieve from all of the giving and extending of ourselves to others, our households, jobs and businesses, churches and professional organizations, should be a priority. "Me" time doesn't have to be a big extravaganza. Simple activities such as walking in a park; staying at home, drinking tea and reading a book or doing absolutely nothing; going to a spa, hanging out with a girlfriend; or taking a long drive are sometimes all that we need to bring a refreshing smile to our souls.

If we neglect to manage our own needs, burnout, resentment, illness, and stress are inevitable. God cannot use us; our family and friends cannot rely on us; our jobs and businesses would suffer; no one would enjoy being around us. Pause for a moment and ask, "Who matters most?" Now say with confidence, "I matter most."

"Me" time clears the mind, relaxes the body, replenishes the soul, and uplifts the spirit. "Me" time refuels us so that we are able to tackle our daily routines with vigor. "Me" time adds peace and balance to our lives. "Me" time reveals to us where we have become crutches to other people and helps us to say "no." "Me" time is a form of self-love.

Let's love ourselves, validate our needs as women, and schedule some "me" time today.

Activities:

1. Sit in silence for 10 minutes.

2. Meditate on today's scripture.

3. Pray and ask God to show you where you have neglected your own needs.

4. Schedule "me" time. You may want to start small by scheduling an hour or two a day of not taking any phone calls, texts, or emails, or participating in any form of social networking. Watch your favorite TV show, read a book, experiment with cooking, exercise, and so on. Do whatever you want; it's your time.

5. Praise God for the ability to treat yourself to some "me" time.

6. Journal about your "me" time experience. How do you feel? Relieved or guilty? If guilty, ask God to remove your guilt and give you peace. Are you ready to make "me" time a regular practice? If no, explain why not.

DAY 20

Being Content

Not that I am referring to being in need; for I have learned to be content with whatever I have. (Philippians 4:11 NRSV)

Some of us are whining, complaining, and comparing ourselves to other women nonstop while sitting in the waiting room. "How much longer?" "When is God coming through for me?" "You said to ask, seek, and knock. I have, and still no husband." "So-and-so just got married. Why haven't I?" "Really, God? I'm 30, 40, 50 years old, and still no husband?"

God hears us, and He truly understands the matters of the heart. We have to be patient and wait. God will not be rushed, nor will He withhold any good thing from us (Psalms 84:11). He simply wants us to be content in the waiting room.

The key to being content is knowing who we are as individuals, where we come from, what we stand for, and what do we ultimately want out of life. When we lack self-knowledge, we find ourselves living with unrest and:

1. orchestrating relational events to occur

2. using Facebook to create our own undercover dating service

3. putting on façades by posing a friend as a lover at a function

4. positioning ourselves in unhealthy places to meet men

5. dating men we really do not like for the sake of having someone

All of this screams, "I'm discontent with my singleness," and it's time to figure out who we really are and why we exist.

This is where looking at the woman in the mirror becomes imperative. It's time for self-reflection, going inward, and asking ourselves thought-provoking questions. And Let's not end there. We must be honest with ourselves when answering those questions. This is a very difficult exercise, but it's very necessary to successfully living a free and fulfilling life.

Some questions we can ask include:

- In whom and what do I believe?

- What are my core values?

- Do I live my life according to my core values and beliefs? If not, why not?

- Who do I say that I am?

- Am I the woman I want to be?

- Who am I becoming?

- Do I repeatedly make the same mistakes? If so, why?

- Do I consistently attract the same kind of man? If so, what kind of man is that? Does this type of man add value to my life or not?

- What is one thing about myself I want to change?

When we know who we are, we can securely show up at an event without a counterfeit fiancé or date on our arm, or proudly choose to stay home. Knowing ourselves equips us to answer the inevitable question, "Why aren't you married yet?" with confidence and honesty. To know oneself is to have an appreciation for our lives, which is at the very heart of being content.

This appreciation means we are living life purposefully, and we are enjoying it. We know that we are single, accept it as a stage in life, and are fine with it. It's in this space that singleness becomes a choice and not a circumstance of life. So, let's choose to be content in the waiting room. A harsh reality is that there are some married women who are figuratively and literally kicking and scratching to get out of their marriages. Intercede on their behalf; pray for their healing, deliverance, and escape, and be content with the here and now.

Activities:

1. Sit in silence for 10 minutes.

2. Meditate on and memorize today's scripture.

3. Journal and ask yourself, "Who am I?" Take some time to answer the previous questions.

4. Pray and ask God to show you how to be content in your singleness. Use today's scripture in your prayer.

5. Schedule some "me" time.

DAY 21

Surrendering

Thy kingdom come. Thy will be done in earth, as it is in heaven. (Matthew 6:10 KJV)

To surrender usually signifies giving up and throwing in the towel, and ultimately losing some sort of fight or competition. However, when it comes to surrendering to God, we actually give in to Him in order to win the race of life.

There is no losing in the Christian life because we are victorious by default. But it can be a game of tug-of-war. God pulls us in one direction, and we pull in the opposite. There are times when we act like spoiled brats and want our way. We kick, scream, act out, and throw tantrums. When that doesn't work, we scheme and try to manipulate God as though He doesn't see and know us. Meanwhile, He sits on His throne, shaking His head and saying to the angels, "Look at my poor baby. She doesn't know the plans that I have for her" (Jeremiah 29:11).

Since we are in the waiting room, it's time for us to abandon unhealthy thought patterns, unforgiveness, pettiness, harmful behaviors, destructive dreams, unproductive conversations, poor habits, and sinful acts. As single women living purposely, it's to our benefit to sever all ties to people, places, things, and activities that hinder our progress in the Lord. Cutting the umbilical cord to everything that goes against God's will, way, and plan isn't easy, but it's very necessary. Besides, those things do not properly nourish our spirits and encourage a life of excellence.

Unnecessary physical and spiritual muscles are exerted when we resist God. We develop six-packs and become strong in the wrong areas. Meanwhile, our spiritual core is limp like spaghetti, and we become easy prey for Satan and his tricks. Our bodies and spirits ache and become dehydrated because we choose not to drink from God's well. And guess what? We suffer loss every time we resist God and do our own thing.

Resisting God by holding on to those things that do not produce fruit in our lives is futile. If God says:

- "No more pity parties"…give them up
- "No more having a live-in partner"…give him up
- "No more maintaining plutonic relationships"…give them up
- "No more cursing and speaking negatively"…give it up
- "No more drinking and partying"…give it up
- "No more living on the fence"…give it up

- "No more lying and being deceptive"…give it up
- "No more controlling and manipulative ways"…give them up
- "No more being critical"…give it up
- "No more masturbating and/or sex outside of marriage"…give it up

To surrender is to love God, and to love God is to obey Him (1 John 5:3). Let's give "it" up, whatever "it" is, and be victorious in the race of life.

Activities:

1. Sit in silence for 10 minutes.

2. Praise God for a few minutes and thank Him for being in your life.

3. Journal whether or not God has revealed to you various aspects of your life that He wants you to give up. List them.

4. Have you surrendered yet? If not, why not?

5. Pray and confess that you are still holding on to certain things. Ask God to forgive you and to give you the discipline to surrender according to His instructions.

6. Schedule some "me" time.

DAY 22

Discernment

Indeed, the word of God is living and active, sharper than any two-edged sword, piercing until it divides soul from spirit, joints from marrow; it is able to judge the thoughts and intentions of the heart. (Hebrews 4:12 NRSV)

Discernment as a spiritual discipline (it's also a spiritual gift) is a divine sense of knowing or understanding. It's the ability to distinguish between who and what is true or false. Some people refer to this spiritual discipline as "women's intuition" or a "sixth sense." However, anyone who consistently prays, fasts, meditates, reads, and studies God's Word and practices silence will inevitably develop a level of discernment.

To have discernment is to also know God's voice. That knowing or understanding that we perceive in our spirits is the Holy Spirit speaking to us. Think back to a time when you said to yourself, "Something told me..." That was God speaking. In general, He speaks in a still, soft voice (1 Kings 19:12). He also speaks in feelings, dreams, and visions. God supernaturally plants life-saving insights into our spirits, and we must trust and obey Him.

God wants us to be happy, but not at the risk of embarrassment, broken hearts, twisted minds, destroyed households, depleted finances, abused on every level, or abandonment at the altar. As we practice discernment, God will equip us to protect our hearts and prevent us from throwing our pearls before swine (Matthew 7:6). In other words, discernment helps us to safeguard all that is precious and special to us – our bodies, hearts, family, dreams, thoughts, emotions, and finances. These are some precious things that are shared in relationships and eventually marriages, but should not necessarily be shared with every man who enters our lives.

So if we feel in our spirits that Michael is not the right man, then it's time to move on. If there is something weird about John and we just cannot put our fingers on it, just walk away. If we have insight that David comes from a line of abusive men, don't give him a second thought. Pray for these men, but keep it moving. Investing time building a relationship after we have discerned the ugly truth about a person is not a smart move.

Today's scripture tells us that God's Word "is able to judge the thoughts and intentions of the heart." Let's remain in God and develop discernment. He will lead us to all that is good and healthy.

Activities:

1. Sit in silence for 10 minutes.

2. Journal an experience when you "knew" that

you should not have gotten involved with a man, but you did anyway. What happened?

3. Were you heartbroken in the end? Are you better now? If so, describe the healing process.

4. Read Matthew 7:6; what does this scripture mean to you? When have you thrown your pearls before swine? Describe the situation and outcome.

5. Pray and ask God to help you sharpen your spiritual senses to make better decisions and to wait for His best.

6. Schedule some "me" time.

DAY 23

Obedience

See, I have set before you today life and prosperity, death and adversity. If you obey the commandments of the Lord your God that I am commanding you today, by loving the Lord your God, walking in his ways, and observing his commandments, decrees, and ordinances, then you shall live and become numerous and the Lord your God will bless you in the land that you are entering to possess. (Deuteronomy 30:15-16 NRSV)

God is our maker and creator, and He knows what is best for us. He created each of us with a specific purpose and has already paved the way for us to bring it to fruition. All God wants from us is unconditional love and our obedience.

To obey, according to the *American Heritage Dictionary*, is to "carry out or fulfill the command, order, or instruction of." Honestly, this is difficult because we all have dreams, desires, plans, goals, and aspirations. Letting go of our agendas and following God, especially when we do not know His plans is very challenging. We cannot see the full picture of what He has in store for us, and that can be unnerving at times. Nevertheless, we must obey Him.

God's way may appear to be unpopular, uncomfortable, unusual, and the opposite of what we want to do. Our duty, though, is to follow God's commands and allow Him to lead us to the place He's envisioned and prepared for us; the Shepherd certainly will not lead His children astray. Satan's plans lead us down the road of destruction. Our plans are fun but always short-lived. But God's plans are to prosper us and not to harm us (Jeremiah 29:11).

When we put aside our rebellious natures and respond properly to God's spirit, we live prosperously. Everything about our lives is in order and thrives. But when we are disobedient, everything that was going right falls to pieces.

Anything that was growing begins decaying. All that was saturated turns dry. What was whole is broken. Whatever was fertile is barren. Go against God's instructions, and death – stress, disease, debt, a broken heart, divorce, unwanted or premature pregnancies, unhealthy relationships, abusive situations, confusion, unemployment, foreclosure, repossessed cars, drama – will come knocking at our front doors.

Obey or disobey. Live or die. God has given us free will to choose. By now, we should know that life is the total of our choices, and each choice we make has its own set of consequences. Let's obey, chose life, and receive prosperity.

Activities:

1. Sit in silence for 10 minutes.

2. Praise God for the power of choice and the ability to choose His way.

3. Journal a prayer asking God to:

   a. show you exactly where you've been disobedient in your life

   b. forgive you

   c. remove your ego and inclination to rebel against Him and others who have authority over you (parents, elders, boss, spiritual leader, government officials, and so on)

   d. teach you to trust, love, and obey Him

4. Research the Bible to find scriptures encouraging us to obey God, and list three.

5. Meditate on the one that most resonates with you and memorize it.

6. Schedule some "me" time.

DAY 24

Biblical Fasting

But when you fast, put oil on your head and wash your face, so that your fasting may be seen not by others but by your Father who is in secret; and your Father who sees in secret will reward you. (Matthew 6:17-18 NRSV)

While in the waiting room, there are times when turning our plates down is very necessary. This activity is best known as fasting.

Biblical fasting is the abstention from food and/or water to get closer to God (contemporary fasting includes abstention from a variety of things). It's an act of worship that requires humility, confession, and repentance. When we fast, we humbly approach God and acknowledge that we have fallen short along our Christian journey.

When fasting, consistent prayer is key, as it complements the fasting experience. Prayer keeps the supernatural communication flowing between God and us. We can pray without fasting, but we can't fast without praying.

The purpose of biblical fasting is to deny ourselves of foods and beverages so that God's spirit can increase within and strengthen us. The denial of self opens the portals of our minds and spirits in such a way that we clearly see Him moving in our lives. Fasting heightens our discernment, and together these disciplines help us to receive clarity, direction, and blessings from God.

This denial of food and beverages also allows us to focus more on God for a spiritual reason than on our fleshly desires and personal needs. Fasting, a voluntary act, should be done with the right motives. It's not a self-centered activity but a God-centered pursuit to tap into that special place of God that we would not otherwise be able to access.

Why should we fast while we are in the waiting room? I have come to learn from personal experiences that even though I may be fasting for a specific reason such as physical healing, God will reveal hidden sins in my life. One time, He pointed out unforgiveness to me, and I quickly confessed and forgave the person. See, fasting can be used as a tool to rid ourselves of sins, bad habits, ungodly behaviors, annoyances, and so forth. These are general personality characteristics that could and eventually will cause strife in a relationship and marriage. So why not eliminate as many of them as possible beforehand?

In today's scripture, Jesus explains to the townspeople that it was unnecessary for his disciples to fast because he was physically with them. Jesus' disciples had a close, personal relationship with Him.

Together, they walked, talked, ate, studied, prayed, healed, and cast out demons. Therefore, fasting was not a necessity.

Jesus isn't physically with us today. Fasting and praying are the tools that we can use to drawer closer to Him and feel His sweet yet powerful presence. So until Jesus returns, we are expected to fast.

Anyone on medication should consult a physician before fasting.

Activities:

1. Research the number of people who fasted in the Bible.

2. List five biblical characters who fasted and why? What was the outcome of their respective fasts?

3. Write out those passages.

4. Pray and ask God to lead you to fast. Ask Him what you should give up and to give you the strength to abstain from it. Also ask Him to lead you to scriptures to read in order to enrich your fasting experience.

5. Remember to remain in prayer while fasting.

DAY 25

Abstinence

"For this reason a man will leave his father and mother and be joined to his wife, and the two will become one flesh." (Ephesians 5:31 NRSV)

While we are on the subject of abstaining, I think it's fitting to touch on sexual abstinence. This spiritual and practical discipline is less popular than biblical fasting. Why wouldn't it be? Sex is healthy and pleasurable, and it's glamorized in every possible way. Sex is on TV and radio commercials, in music and music videos, movies, video games, and the Internet. Yes, sex is highly promoted, but singles are precluded from having sex — and for good reason.

Sex, like everything else on earth, has its purpose and place in this life. A husband and wife are able to participate in sexual relations to procreate, express love, make up, have fun, and enjoy each other. This beautiful and powerful activity is not to be used recreationally but responsibly and in the proper context – marriage.

Today, God is calling for all singles to abstain from sex, not to punish us, but to protect us. It's clear that men and women are joined together physically during sex. But are you aware that a spiritual connection occurs while having sex? The scripture at the beginning of this devotion tells us that we become one. Two bodies and two spirits connect and are united. That is deep!

Our physical forms, emotions, and attitudes merge and become knitted together. We become a part of them, and they become a part of us. An intense bond takes shape and lasts indefinitely.

It's very possible that months or maybe years after breaking up with an ex-boyfriend or ex-lover, our bodies will still crave that man. Then he surprisingly calls "out of the blue" – at least that's what we think. Have you ever experienced this?

Maybe it's because during sex we share all of ourselves with that person in the physical, emotional, and spiritual realms. An intense level of intimacy is reached through sex that ties our spirits, minds, emotions, and bodies together, an intimacy that would not otherwise occur. This creates a powerful level of *knowing* each other that may very well exist for some time, which may explain why, post-breakup, our spirits, minds, emotions, and bodies call out to each other. And although we really do not want to re-establish a relationship with that person, our spirits, minds, emotions, and bodies *want* to reconnect and relive the moments we once shared.

This deep connection reminds me of the scripture that says, "Deep calls to deep" (Psalms 42:7). God calls out to the deep places of our hearts, spirits, and souls. Why? Because He is more than just familiar with us, He *knows* us because He created us and our innermost being.

Nothing about us is hidden from God, and everything about us is precious to Him like exquisite jewels. Not everyone is privileged or worthy enough to experience the deepness of our existences. There are places on reserve only for our husbands, and no part of us is off limits to God. His touch brings about healing, deliverance, and blessings.

The first time I felt God leading me to practice abstinence, I thought surely He meant that word for someone else. It was not possible for God to be talking to me — at least, that is what I wanted to believe. But time progressed, and I surrendered to the Lord's will, not fully understanding why He wanted me to practice abstinence. Sure, I was aware of what the Word says about sex outside of marriage, but I didn't *get it* until I started to *live it*. When we live in sin, going against what God requires, we create a disconnect between God and us, thereby limiting our ability to live freely and be great at all we do.

While we wait for God to bless us with a husband, it's to our advantage to be intimate with Him. Intimate in the sense that we talk with Him, pray to Him, fast, journal, meditate, practice silence – *know* Him. When His spirit calls out to us, we are certain that it's for good reason, and we can willingly respond. Our heavenly Father will keep us while we wait, and extend His grace to prevent us from giving into temptation, living in sin, and creating a disconnect between Him and us.

Activities:

1. List the number of times that you regretted having sex as a single woman. Why, what happened each time?

2. Have you ever thought about an ex and he "just showed up?" Describe the situation. Did the two of you reunite? If so, in what way?

3. Locate and jot down as many scriptures as possible that speak against fornication. Commit to memorizing at least three of these scriptures. Hide them in your heart.

4. Pen a prayer asking God to show you how to abstain from sex and to save your private jewels until He blesses you with a husband.

5. Fasting for a few days is a really good way to begin practicing abstinence.

6. If you are already practicing abstinence, ask God to continue to strengthen you in this area. Intercede on behalf of someone you know who is having a difficulty time with abstaining from sex.

Be encouraged. You can do this.

DAY 26

Being Grateful

Then one of them, when he saw that he was healed, turned back, praising God with a loud voice. He prostrated himself at Jesus' feet and thanked him… (Luke 17:15-16 NRSV)

Being grateful is an act of humility. It shows that we know without a shadow of doubt that it is God providing for and covering us. By saying "thank you" we acknowledge Him, His goodness, power, and love. God looks out for each of us and meets our needs, nurtures our souls, and loves us endlessly. We live, move, and have our being because of God (Acts 17:28).

Take 60 seconds to think back over our lives to when God:

- delivered us from a reckless lifestyle of partying, drinking, driving under the influence, having recreational sex, etc.

- extended his grace to keep us from committing suicide when life was too much to bear

- guided our footsteps home to our families after a hard day of work

- pulled us through surgery totally healed and not damaged from contaminated or left-behind tools

- granted us traveler's mercy from our homes to the corner of our blocks; from state to state; from country to country; from continent to continent

God is incredibly awesome and amazing. He deserves a BIG thank you right now. Thank Him for being in the waiting room. Being here means that He has kept us from men and relationships that are harmful, superficial, incompatible, and unhealthy, and which do not glorify him. Thank Him for not being unhappily married and seeking a way of escape.

Today we are taking a stand to no longer worry and complain about anything, especially our marital status. We are conditioning our minds to always be grateful for:

- all that we have and do not have

- the ability to blink our eyes and wiggle our fingers and toes

- the ability to brush our teeth and dress ourselves on our own

- the small things

- the love of family and friends

These and all blessings from God deserve a heartfelt "thank you."

Activities:

1. Sit in silence for 10 minutes.

2. Journal a time when God came through for you and you forgot to say "thank you." Pen a prayer confessing, apologizing, and thanking Him now. Then ask God to remind you each day to say "thank you" for the small things.

3. List all of the things that you are grateful for.

DAY 27

Trusting God

...In great fear the Israelites cried out to the Lord. They said to Moses, "Was it because there were no graves in Egypt that you have taken us away to die in the wilderness? What have you done to us, bringing us out of Egypt? Is this not the very thing we told you in Egypt, 'Let us alone and let us serve the Egyptians'? For it would have been better for us to serve the Egyptians than to die in the wilderness." (Exodus 14:10-13 NRSV)

A stronghold is a negative spirit that keeps us in bondage and tied to people, things, habits, behaviors, cultures and lifestyles that are not befitting for us as God's children. Strongholds limit our ability to progress and move forward into the future that God planned for us. Fear is a weighty stronghold that stops us from trusting God.

Fear stirs up just the right amount of doubt, apprehension, worry, and concern to entice us to return to what used to be. Like the Israelites who preferred to return to a life of slavery instead of trusting God, we sometimes go back to our past. We make contact with ex-boyfriends and ex-lovers instead of trusting God to bless us with the husband He prepared for us.

Friends, let's be honest: There were times we pursued our past in the midst of boredom and loneliness. The cell phone was next to us, and the laptop was within arm's reach. Thoughts about past relationships saturated our minds. We remembered when…when we had a movie date, dinner companion, someone to talk with all night long, a buddy to flirt with, a man…a man who courted and protected us, stimulated our minds, made us laugh and feel good and loved us.

Our thoughts, the phone, and Internet are a deadly combination when we are home alone, bored and lonely. We start scheming and playing back in our minds the "good times" and how to reinvent those moments. Then the texting, emailing, calling, and reaching out to ex-boyfriends or ex-lovers online begin. This is fear in action. We are fearful that we will never date again and we do not trust God enough to not extend Him a helping hand.

It's in these desperate times that we have be deliberate about trusting God. How? Well, by praying. Praying? I'll be the first to admit that this is a difficult assignment. Who wants to pray when the desires of our hearts are spilling over into what appears to be an empty well? Who can pray when the flesh is weak? Why pray when God can easily send our husbands?

Psalms 55:22 tells us, "Cast your burden on the Lord, and He will sustain you; He will never permit the righteous to be moved." We have to learn to tell God how much what we are going through hurts and trust Him to come through for us. He will give us peace to ease our minds and get us through any temporary difficult time.

I recall being home, bored and lonely one evening. I was watching the Word Network and a commercial for a Christian online dating service appeared. It caught my attention. Naturally, I flipped open my MacBook and pulled up the website. As I perused the site looking for anyone who physically appealed to me, I felt God telling me to disconnect from the site. I obeyed because I knew that I was about to start some mess and then beg God to get me out of it. Have you been here before?

Not only did I get offline and shut my MacBook down, but I also pulled out my Bible; I needed something promising to sustain me in the midst of my loneliness, boredom, and mistrust of God. I randomly opened the Bible to Isaiah, and Isaiah 54:5 was the verse that arrested my attention. It reads, "For your Maker is your **husband**, the Lord of hosts is His name;" That Word blew my mind. I quickly journaled what it meant to me in that moment and was free of the fear of being alone for the rest of my life.

God sends us promises to remind us of who He is so that we can wholeheartedly trust Him. Remember that Jesus walked the earth in the flesh. He is well acquainted with human emotions and desires, and he empathizes with each of us. One day, God will bless us with our hearts' desires. But until then, let's cast our cares upon Him and trust Him with all of our might to:

- be our husband in the interim (Isaiah 54:5)
- bring the right man into our lives at the right time
- comfort and keep us during our loneliness
- keep us focused on the future and not the past
- steer us away from men who do not mean us well

Activities:

1. Sit in silence for 10 minutes.

2. Pray and ask God to increase your trust in Him and to remove all fear from your heart. Ask God to help you to look forward and not backward.

3. Read, meditate, and memorize Isaiah 54:5. Journal: What does it mean that God is your husband? What are the attributes of a husband?

DAY 28

Faithfulness

Know therefore that the Lord your God is God, the faithful God who maintains covenant loyalty with those who love him and keep his commandments, to a thousand generations…(Deuteronomy 7:9 NRSV)

All throughout the Old Testament, God likened His relationship with the Israelites to a marriage between a man and woman. He loved the Israelites with an everlasting love and was faithful to the entire nation. God provided manna when they were hungry, kept their shoes from wearing out, and turned a stone into water to quench their thirst while they were in the desert. He was their sun by day and moon by night; He never left them.

On the other hand, the Israelites left God in their hearts numerous times because they were impatient with Him. Like some of us, the Israelites wanted God to always make their lives comfortable and trouble free. When the Israelites didn't immediately get their way, they committed spiritual adultery by creating gods of silver and gold (Isaiah 31:7). In pursuit of instant gratification, they practiced idolatry and served breathless gods

– gods that could not walk, talk, give life, save, heal, or deliver.

Today, some of us are practicing idolatry. There are some activities, things, or people that we are devoting an inordinate amount of time to instead of to God, especially during trying times. Our careers, weight, body image, material possessions, social media, food, and marital status have become the objects of our affection.

These gods have taken first place in some of our lives and have become substitutions for the real deal – God. They help us to avoid reality and give us a false sense of hope and satisfaction when life is challenging and difficult. To our detriment, we seek solace in these gods and defile ourselves.

We become dirty, despicable, intolerable, and hated by God when we practice idolatry (Deuteronomy 16:22) – when we worship things and people other than God. In addition, we break the commandments that tell us "…you shall have no other gods before Me" and "You shall not make for yourself an idol, whether in the form of anything that is in the heaven above or that is on the earth beneath, or that is in the water under the earth." (Exodus 20:3-4 NRSV) Idolatry is a sin.

God requires true covenant with each of us. It's a one-on-one relationship that He wants, no substitutions and no additional parties. Whenever we are ugly, unlovable, fake, phony, selfish, arrogant, foolish, or miserable, God doesn't walk out on us and seek replacements or other children to love. He remains with us and lovingly corrects us. Our heavenly Father is loyal, trustworthy, and faithful to His children no matter what, and God wants the same level of faithfulness in return while we are in the waiting room.

Being in the waiting room can be challenging at times because life will throw us a curve ball or two. We will become lonely, which is a fact of life. Fear of not having a husband will rise up in us periodically. Desires for sexual pleasure will certainly make an appearance, however often. But we cannot turn to food, the Internet, sex, money, shopping or anything else or person other than God for satisfaction, freedom, completeness or attention.

Be faithful to and worship God *only* in the waiting room and beyond.

Activities:

1. Sit in silence for 10 minutes.

2. Read and meditate on Exodus 20:3-4.

3. How has being unfaithful manifested in your life? Have you cheated on an ex-boyfriend? When, why and for how long?

4. What idols/gods have you created in your life? Why?

5. Was there ever a time when you felt like God

was unfaithful to you? Describe the situation. Do you still feel that way today? If so, why?

6. Pray and ask God to forgive you for being unfaithful in past relationships. Ask Him to forgive you for creating idols in your life. Forgive God if you've felt that He turned his back on you and left you behind. Ask God to renew your relationship with Him and to give you wisdom to seek Him only. Ask God to continue to build up your character so that you will remain faithful to your husband and vice versa during difficult times.

DAY 29

Fellowshipping

...we declare to you what we have seen and heard so that you also may have fellowship with us; and truly our fellowship is with the Father and with his son Jesus Christ. (1 John 1:3 NRSV)

The word fellowship, according to *Webster's*, means "companionship and company." When we spend time with God – when we pray, read the Word, journal, fast, and the like – we become His companions and vice versa. *Webster's* also defines fellowship as "a community of interest and a company of equals or friends: association." It's our Christian duty to be in fellowship with a body of Christian believers, especially while we are single; we need to be accountable to others for our spiritual lives.

As Christians we are expected to join a church where we can grow spiritually and work out our souls' salvation. Keep in mind that any church will not do. The name doesn't have to be long and filled with several biblical clichés. Denomination and size do not matter, either. The most important matter is that the leader of the church believes in and knows God and is teaching and preaching Jesus Christ.

Church connects us to like-minded people who are just as imperfect as we are and committed to God's ways. There are no perfect churches because there are no perfect people. Pastors are not perfect, and neither are ministers, officers, members, and visitors. Each of us has sinned and continues to sin. Our common need for God is what brings us together under one roof to learn, mature, be healed, delivered, and transformed to do the work that God called each of us to do.

Being a member of a church exposes us to the Word, increases our faith, teaches us how to serve others and corporately worship God, and gives us a sense of belonging and responsibility. Church reminds us that we are not on this Christian journey alone and there are others whom we can call upon when in need of sound Christian advice and prayer. Fellowshipping and going to church while in the waiting room reminds us that we are part of God's family.

Activities:

1. If you do not have a church home, pray and ask God to lead you to the church He wants you to join.

2. If you have a church home but for whatever reasons stopped going, ask God to give you strength to return to that church or find a new

church. If you had a bad church experience, journal what happened and forgive the people involved.

3. If you are skeptical about joining a church, ask God to remove your skepticism and increase your trust in Him. Ask God to open your heart and spirit to receive the truth and the church He has in mind for you.

4. Ask God to send you a husband who will not only enthusiastically attend church with you and discuss the Word with you but who will also take his rightful place in your home, church, on his job, community and the world.

DAY 30

Waiting

From ages past no one has heard, no ear has perceived, no eye has seen any God besides you, who works for those who wait for Him. (Isaiah 64:4 NRSV)

While we wait it should be with hope and anticipation that God will come through for us in the way that we desire. Waiting takes patience, strength, and wisdom. It builds character and matures and stretches us in unbelievable ways.

God is generous and every good and perfect gift comes from Him (James 1:17). This tells us that any husband from God is worth the wait. God is working as we wait for the right husband to appear. God has already molded and shaped our husbands-to-be. Now God is preparing us to recognize and receive our gift. This waiting journey may come with some imposters, sheep in wolves clothing, and we need to be able to quickly discern, recognize, and cancel them out.

It's in the wait that God removes traces of desperation and naïveté from us to prevent us from awakening love too soon (Solomon 3:5). When we awaken love too soon, we forget about our boundaries and give away pieces of ourselves to someone who doesn't deserve us. He will play games with our minds and hearts and have us twisted and confused. This is not characteristic of the marriage God has in mind for us.

God will certainly fulfill our desires to be married and to have a lifelong partner (if that is His will). The husband that God blesses us with will create a marriage that is the epitome of true covenant as a testimony of our faithful God. We will have a marriage that represents, mirrors, values, and glorifies God.

So how do we wait for God to bless us according to our desires? We praise, worship, love, trust, and obey Him. We develop a closer relationship with Him by practicing spiritual and practical disciplines on a daily basis. We wait with patience, endurance, humility, and expectancy. We wait with our eyes opened and focused on God. We wait for our name to be called. We purposefully and freely wait.

Activities:

1. Meditate on today's scripture.

2. Journal what it means to you.

3. Pray and thank God for introducing you to or reminding you of spiritual and practical disciplines. Ask God to give you strength and maturity to wait for the right husband, no matter how challenging the wait becomes. Ask God to strengthen you to continue to practice these disciplines every day.

DAY 31

Renewing The Mind

Summing it all up, friends, I'd say you'll do best filling your minds and meditating on things true, noble, reputable, authentic, compelling, gracious – the best, not the worst; the beautiful, not the ugly; things to praise, not things to curse. Put into practice what you learned from me, what you heard and saw and realized. Do that, and God who makes everything work together will work you into His most excellent harmonies (Philippians 4:8-9 The Message).

Renewing the mind is a process that can and will be accomplished while sitting in the waiting room. This process begins with elevating our thinking. We have to consciously shift from habitually thinking on nonsense and negativity to deliberately focusing on things that are progressive, true, righteous, and positive. These are nuggets of repair and rebirth that only add value to our lives and take us to new heights in God.

It's important that we censor the music we listen to, the TV programs we watch, the books and magazines we read, the games we play, and the places we frequent. All of these activities influence our thinking and therefore our behavior. Whatever we feed on will eventually be revealed in our conversations and decision-making. It's like eating with our mouths open. Everyone can see all that we have taken in – the garbage that we consume will be highly visible to others. The only way to prevent it from spewing out of our pores and giving off a foul stench is to change our mental, physical, and spiritual diets. The Bible tells us that as a man thinks so is he (Proverbs 23:7).

How do we renew our minds? First, we renew our minds by learning God's Word and applying it to our lives. It's not enough to immerse ourselves in the Word and know it; we have to live it on a daily basis. By living God's Word our thoughts and actions will steadily become aligned with God's ways.

Second, we have to eliminate everything and everyone from our lives that does not add value and enhance our lives. There are places, habits, vices, and people that can and will rob us of our greatness, which is not what God intends for us.

Third, it's extremely important for us to surround ourselves with God-knowing people, positive individuals, folk who are doing better than we are, sisters and brothers who have personal or professional skills we want to acquire and hone, people who have a different perspective on life, individuals who are pursuing excellence. The bottom line is that we should seek the Lord and all His ways and keep company with people who are living right-eously and are making positive contributions to their families and communities.

Activities:

1. Sit in silence.

2. Pray that God will give you the desire and dis-cipline to renew your mind.

3. Journal and ask God to reveal to you those hab-its, music selections, TV shows, reading mate-rials, and people that you need to rid yourself of. Ask Him which spiritual and practical dis-ciplines should you engage more frequently in respect to renewing your mind.

4. Journal and ask God to show you the areas of your life where you are not applying His Word.

5. Journal and ask God to point out to you each time you think negatively or irresponsibly and do not add value to your life or the lives of oth-ers.

6. Praise God for the first day of your new habit of exercising spiritual and practical disciplines. Yea!

SALVATION

Prayer Of Faith

So, you are not a Christian, and God moved on your heart while going through this devotional to give your life to Christ? All you have to do is say:

I confess with my lips that Jesus is Lord and I believe in my heart that God raised Him from the dead (Romans 10:9).

If you said the above and believe it, you are saved. *(Journal this experience so that you will never forget it.)*

Welcome to God's royal family!

Bibliography

I used the following books as guides to write The Waiting Room:

Calhoun, A. (2005). Spiritual Disciplines, Practices That Transform Us. Illinois: Intervarsity Press

Ellis-Smith, M.A., Jackson, F.W., Logan, P., Church, C. (Eds.). (1991).

Holman Bible Dictionary. Tennessee: Holman Dictionary Publishers

Kingston, K. (1999). Clear Your Clutter with Feng Shui. New York: Random House

Neufeldt, V. Guralnik, D. (Eds). (1988) New World Dictionary (3rd ed). New York: Simon & Schuster, Inc.

ABOUT THE AUTHOR

T.C. Spellen is an independent author, speaker, workshop facilitator, and mentor.

TC is passionate about leading single women in living a purposeful life through practicing spiritual and practical disciplines. She enjoys "real talk" and looks forward to having "real talk" with other single women to address the challenges of singleness.

TC is a Christian woman who not only enjoys reading the Bible but also applies it to her life. She attends church on Sundays and is an active member who serves on a few ministries. Traveling, eating, listening to music, going to spas, catching up with friends, and reading murder mysteries are some of her hobbies.

Since her undergraduate days, TC aspired to write a book. With every life issue, the topic changed, and with each attempt to begin writing she was confused, fearful, and self-defeated. But God removed her fears, gave her clarity, and opened the right door at the right time. Now single women across the globe have a guide for how to live while waiting for God's very best to show up.

To connect with and/or follow T.C. Spellen:

Email:
TCSpellen@TCSpellen.com

Facebook:
www.facebook.com/pages/TCSpellen/29192392091
7825

Twitter:
Twitter.com/TCSpellen

Smashwords:
www.smashwords.com/profile/view/TCSpellen

Thank you for purchasing and reading *The Waiting Room*.

Walk In Your Dreams!

35949753R00071

Made in the USA
San Bernardino, CA
08 July 2016